# Coalville
## as I remember it

Edited by Louise Oglesby

Belvoir Road, Coalville.

**Leicestershire Libraries & Information** *Service*

*a Leicestershire County Council publication*

© Leicestershire Libraries and Information Service 1988

First published 1988. Leicestershire Libraries and Information Service, Thames Tower, Navigation Street, Leicester LE1 3TZ.

Designed by Clare Wallin.

Typeset by Echo Press (1983) Ltd.

Printed by Echo Press (1983) Ltd.

ISBN 0850222524

All rights reserved. No part of this publication may be photocopied, recorded or otherwise reproduced, stored in a retrieval system or transmitted in any form or by any electronic or mechanical means without the prior permission of the copyright owner.

# Introduction

"Coalville As I Remember It" was the title of a creative writing competition organised by Leicestershire Libraries and Information Service during the summer, 1987. Previous competitions had already been held in the Belgrave and West End areas of Leicester, Melton Mowbray and Lutterworth.

People were invited to submit their written or taped memories of the Coalville area (including the surrounding villages of Bardon, Hugglescote, Ravenstone, Swannington, Thringstone and Whitwick, as well as the town of Coalville itself) before 1950.

Over forty entries were received, two of which were on tape, and because of the high standard it was decided that five prizes would be awarded, in no order of merit.

Because "Coalville As I Remember It" was a creative writing competition, the judges were not primarily concerned with historical accuracy, but were looking for enjoyable, readable accounts of personal memories and experiences.

This book contains a selection of those memories. It is divided into two parts. The first contains the edited scripts of the five prizewinners; the second contains as many extracts from the other scripts as space would allow. These extracts have been arranged into the following subject areas:
Social Life; Shopping; Work; The War Years; Schooldays.

# Acknowledgements

Mrs. Grace Cox, Librarian who spent much time and effort in publicising the competition.
Mantle Community Arts, Springboard Centre, Coalville, who assisted in the organisation and publicity.
Mantle Oral History Project, Springboard Centre, Coalville, who very kindly donated prizes.
The judges: Mr. Haywood, Coalville Citizens Advice Bureau; Mrs. J. Sheehan, formerly Coalville Age Concern; Mr. D. Baker, lecturer and local historian.
Above all those people who took part in "Coalville As I Remember It", for their varied and fascinating collection of memories.

MRS. M. PAGE was born in North Street (now Central Road), Hugglescote, and was one of the five prizewinners.
She remembers Coalville after the First World War, and provides a fascinating picture of family and community life at that time.

"After the war, we always went to Coalville on Saturday afternoons; it was a treat for us. Outside the station wall, a lot of wreaths were laid to form graves in memory of those who got killed fighting and a lot of people were looking at them with tears in their eyes.

After looking round them we went round the shops. The Penny Bazaar was one we liked to go in because we usually got something from there to finish our outing. We would call at the Co-op cafe, which was next to the Primitive Chapel; there we would have a fancy cake and a drink. We were fascinated by the way the money went back and forward in little boxes which fitted on a pully. They pulled a handle and it went along wires into the grocery department, then came back with the change; to us it was very interesting.

Empire Day celebrations, Bridge Road School, Coalville, 1937.

I went to Bridge Road School (which is now the Tech.). Empire Day was a big event every year when the girls would be dressed in white, the boys in black knee length trousers, white shirts, white or black gym shoes. Some would dance round the maypole, others do exercises. We would all sing together "Land of Hope and Glory", also "God Bless the Prince of Wales" and others. It was very enjoyable; our parents would come to watch as well. Another big day in our lives was the unveiling of the memorial which is still in front of the school. All the children marched round to the front, all in white for a service to the teachers who lost their lives. Mr. J. H. Massey was the headmaster, it has always remained as one of the most memorable days.

My father worked at the pit and was mostly on night shift. On light nights we would go so far with him which took us to the brook where he would stop on the bridge to fill his bottle from the spring, which was ice cold. He would also take in what he called his "snap bag" two very thick slices of bread and a lump of cheese.

His bag was made of calico and it was always spotlessly clean. He came home next morning as black as soot, (there were no baths then) he also came home very often wet through; then his clothes had to be dried before he went on the next shift.

Pigeons were a hobby with my father, so racing was a big thing with him. When the racing season was on he would come home from work, change his trousers but still with his black face, would get one of us up. (We did it in turn). He put the birds in a basket and carried it down to Hugglescote station, then put the birds on the train, then they would be taken to different places, then be released to fly back home. Dad would buy a bun for us going home from Smith's bakers shop on Porters Corner.

Often we would be wakened by men who came to empty the closets we called them, (which are toilets). They were like a tin box with a wooden top and a hole in the middle. It would be the flashing lights from their lamps which woke us up. These closets we shared between two families who kept it clean in turns.

Once a month Dad had a load of coal which was tipped up on the roadside. Many a time we had to get the barrow and get in the coalhouse, it was hard work. We also would have to fetch soft water from a pump which was in the middle of the row of houses, to put in the boiler for hot water, then we would get it out with a ladle which was like a tin with a handle on to wash us with and anything else which needed hot water.

A special event for the neighbours was when there was a pig to be killed. Everyone in the row took part. They would all put the coppers on for hot water to make scraping the hairs of the pig easier. A man would come in gaiters and have on a big apron, a lot of knives and a bier to put the pig on. After the animal was killed, it was cut up and shared, someone would make pork pie, someone else make sausages, the bellys would be turned by some other person. Lard was also rendered down and shared up. What the children liked most was the bladder which was dried then blowed up for a football. The lady who made the pork pie was also the lady who laid out the people who died.

On holidays from school a treat for us would be a picnic at Forest Rock. We would have some food packed up, then walk up to Spring Hill. It was an awful long way but we enjoyed it. After the picnic we picked heather and bilberries, which we had later in a pie. On the way home we called at the Forest Rock for a rest and a drink then carried on home tired but happy.

Fairs were also an event when they came. It was fun trying all the rides; my favourite was the cake walk. On Sunday afternoon there would be an organ recital and lots of people went to hear it with their families.

Sunday school was something we had to do, we went morning and evening. After the service, we went for a walk then back home to sing hymns in the firelight.

Flower shows were something everyone enjoyed. It would be a full day out, gardeners would be getting the stuff in the allotments months before the show. It was a great time. Also, once a year, we had the Co-op Treat. We would march from our own village with a band, then join the other villages to have tea on the Co-op field. We would take our own mugs; the co-op would give us a bag with food in.

The only time I have ever seen Marlborough Square full of people was when Lloyd George came to the Liberal Club. I think everybody in Coalville turned out to hear him from the balcony of the club.

I started to work when I was fourteen at Burgess Elastic factory, making knicker elastic. It was a dirty job but there were no other jobs. After a week's work I received eight shillings and threepence, of which my mother gave me the three pence for pocket money. I went to the pictures for twopence, then had a pennyworth of chips going home. Later I had a rise in my wages, so then I had a shilling to spend. I still went to the pictures, but then I could have some sweets to take in with me and some mushy peas with my chips, and a cup of Oxo.

Burgess Cord and Braid Shop, 1928.

When we went to work, we did not get up with alarm clocks — the buzzers from the pit woke everyone roundabout. It told the miners what time it was, either to go home, or go to work. If the buzzers went on for a little while, people would know there had been an accident down the mine.

I was twenty three when I met my husband. War was declared on September 3rd 1939, so we decided to get married on the 30th September. After the wedding, when we had paid all our expenses, we had half a crown (two shillings and sixpence) left to live on for the rest of the week. My husband was working at the pit. They were on short time then, working only three days on and three days off which he had the dole for. Our wages for the week was £1.11 shillings; good money down the pits came later.

As the war got worse, planes were coming over, dropping bombs anywhere, everybody had to black out all windows, doors, anywhere where there was a chink of light. I was expecting my first baby in 1941. The sirens went one night after we had gone to bed and all of a sudden we heard such a bang — it rocked the bed so much we thought we had been hit. My husband jumped over me, ran down stairs, put on his Home Guard uniform, ran down the street to other men already on duty, and left me to struggle as best I could. Two bombs were dropped close by that night, and made an enormous hole.

Rationing was a problem, but people helped each other then by swapping things they did not want, e.g. if someone had fat they would swap that to someone else who had something they wanted. It was terrible to go out at night, there were no lights anywhere, it was pitch black, specially in the winter.

We got through the war; I had two sons who grew up like other children. This is the time everything started to change — people were getting more money, children were getting more and more, they did not make their own amusements any more. Now I know this account is not very exciting to anyone else, but it was what we had, and we enjoyed it at the time and I don't think it did us any harm."

---

JOAN BROTHERHOOD BLACKEY now lives in Auckland, New Zealand, but she has not forgotten her childhood in the nineteen-thirties: rides in Grandad's pony and trap, Grey Carrs fever powders, and Condy's Crystals, playing "Tin-a-Lurkie" on Thringstone Green, and picking bilberries up near Spring Hill. Joan was another prizewinner, and an unusual feature of her entry was that it was in the form of two poems.

---

## Gone, but not forgotten

Aspidistra's and Antimaccassors,
In Grandma Rossell's front room.
The Pig cage that dropped through the Coalmine's bottom,
filling Coalville with gloom.
Steedman's teething powders and "Ippikeckianna"
Two pennorth of four ha'porths,

for we couldn't afford a tanner.
Jeyes Fluid and Condy's Crystals that coloured boiling water,
Threepennorth of Infants preservative,
to quiet a son or daughter.
Blue Bags to whiten the washing,
Dolly Bags for curtain nets.
OXYDOL and RINSO and ACDO Square all gets
The brightest wash you ever did see.
When used in the Dolly Tub
With the punchers and the Dolly Pegs
So you didn't have much to rub.
The Big Zinc bath by the fireside
In which we tried to swim.
White Windsor soap, that floated on water
Fulfilling our nautical whim.
Carter's Little Liver Pills,
Curtains made of serge,
Dandelion and Burdock, that often felt the urge
Fancy Tortoise shell hairpins,
We wore Navy Reefer Jackets.
Hundreds and thousands on worm cakes,
that were sold in little packets.
The clothes line then, was made of wire
or else of plaited string,
With a fire under the copper,
We drank water from Bob's closs Spring.
There was Goose Grease and Sloan's linament
If you suffered with "The Screws"
No TV or No Radio, but we read the "Reynolds News"
Sometimes if I was lucky,
and could "get one ovver me betters,"
I might be able to sneak a look,
at me Grannie B's "Red Letters".
Ink in tiny china pots,
and scratchy steel pen knibs,
Vests and 'Commbs' of purest wool to cover the skinniest
ribs.
Paraffin lamps to read by, as we sat in the warm living room,
Or the glow of a little wax candle,
to light up the bedrooms' gloom.
Softening salt in a Big Brown Bag
To make the hard water smooth,
The Black Beaded cape and bonnet,
that was worn by Mrs. Booth.
Facepowder and rouge, made by Windbloom,
that gave off a lovely scent,
Evening in Paris and Mischief,
that the year before you had meant,
to give to your friends for a present, for the glorious Yuletide
season,

but, when you'd opened the little screw cap — well —
It really stands to reason,
That the perfume could be wasted
On such an indifferent friend,
So now that you've "oppenned the bottle"
You'll just keep it in the end.
Don't forget ya Ganzie, for it's perishing outside
and if it kaips on freezing, you'll be able to
Mek a slide —
Sherbert Dabs and Gobstoppers, Everlasting toffee strip
Navy bloomers were bought with a pocket stitched on
And that Pinna, you'd managed to rip.
The sofa was stuffed with horsehair,
and upholstered with real leather,
You tried, so hard to sit, but you kept slipping off
Till right at the end of your tether,
You'd slide down onto the living room floor,
to sit on the old pegged rug,
Reading a County Library book, drinking cocoa from Dad's
big mug.
In front of a glowing fire,
and there you would remain,
Till you tiptoed up the "Wooden Hill"
To jump into cold "Sheet Lane."
The Big Brass Bed was work of art
Screwed onto a wire frame, the
Mattress, that was filled with flock,
and that needed turning again.
Jones came from Leicester,
and we bought their Ginger Pop
In a big brown pottery bottle,
with a stopper in the top.
There were births and deaths and marriages
Just like there are today,
But after the wedding breakfast,
you might not afford to go away,
If the marriage too was a failure,
No use to rant and rave.
"Yen madeya bed, ya mun lie on it."
That was the advice others gave.
If we went for a ride round the forest,
Grandad lent us the pony and trap
The pony knew his own way home,
so we had no need of a map.
We didn't have a wardrobe, just a curtain across the corner,
A heavy marbled topped washstand,
Dad's black tie, we would lend to a mourner.
Lovely Bedroom china, trimmed with pretty little flowers,
no such place as a bathroom, or the quickness of showers.

I've remembered Mulford Violets and Phulnana's Perfume too,
and those little scented floral gums
That were much too hard to chew.
June wasn't only a month of the year
It was also a Bottle of Scent,
There were corsets and Liberty Bodices
and the board that said "Repent"
that the man in the old fawn raincoat,
carried about the town.
The warning voice that told you
"Kaip aweey from Stabbs Pond or ya'll drown!"
The Ice-cream man who pedalled around as he shouted
"Hokey Pokey!"
Dancing the Veleeta before the days of Hokey Cokey.
Yes! I think I could write for hours of those days, that have long since gone,
when you and I were very young
Back in Nineteen thirty one,
so in jogging your faded memory,
I hope I've made you smile,
and it's brightened your busy work a day world,
perhaps for a little while.
As you've entered the Age of retirement,
though you still may be feeling 'amazed'.
Be thankful you live in these modern times,
But remember those Good Old Days.

The Roundabout, Coalville, 1950's.

# Was it really like this?

It seems so long since I went away
And Oh! what a change I've seen
The grass seemed so much greener then
When I played on Thringstone Green
Old homes have gone, old faces too
Have long since passed away
In fact it all seems smaller now
than in my yesterday.
There's no Midland Red Bus
Now driving to Lount
Conveying the Miner to Pit
To hew the coal for a Blazing Fire
As snug and warm we'd sit
on that cosy handpegged hearth rug
As we "Drank" our OXO cubes
Or with croaking voice and aching throat
We had "Scoffed" a Tin of ZUBES
Or that tiny box of minute black squares
I think we called them "NIPS"
Sucking vinegar thru a paper bag
After eating a "Pennorth o' chips"
Jack Frost gave us the "hot aches"
The summer sun sent one brown
Curling up on the sofa
'neath a feather eiderdown.
The gathering of the blackberries
with which to make jelly or jam
Picking Bilberries up near Spring Hill farm, and then tipping up
the can,
So those small and juicy little fruits
Lay all scattered and all squashed
As our juice strained teeth and purple mouth
That no matter how we washed,
Would always give the game away
That most bilberries we had eaten.
Nev'r mind, "Tomorrow's just another day"
So I'm sure we won't be beaten.
Fishing for tiddlers down at The Brook
The water soon got murky
Then back at night on Thringstone Green
As we played at "Tin a Lurkie".
Strolling down the Woodside
To gather the bits of wood
That lit the fire on Bonfire Night
Oh didn't that feel good!
We would finish off the "Black Ball"
That seemed much to hard to bite.
New frocks for sermons Sunday
Wasn't that a pretty sight?

Do you remember Vimto
Or the Bun at the Co-op Treat?
when after walking from Village to Coalville
We would sit with aching feet
In a field at the Top of Ashby Road
Just down round the Ravenstone Turn!
The milk wasn't sold in bottles then
It came in a great big churn.
Then was "doled out" in smaller measure
From a heavy lidded pail.
Oh yes, I know I'm rambling on,
But I'm getting old and frail!
So while looking back on My Memories
and comparing with things that are new
or the many changing scenes of life
That have long since faded from view.
I recall with fond affection
Childhood joys that are long since past
Looking on to that bright tomorrow
And those Memories that last,
As back to New Zealand I travel
From the things that I still hold dear
May you Remember Me,
As I Remember You
Dear Village of yesteryear.

Another prizewinner MRS. KATHLEEN M. DONALDSON contributed some recollections of life in Hugglescote in the 1920s. She vividly portrays the changes which were taking place, with the health service, the coming of electricity and radio, and their effect on daily life.

"At the end of the First World War I was 6 years old. I have therefore only a few, very hazy recollections of that time, of the ghostly searchlights seeking out some lurking Zeppelin over Loughborough, of adults talking in lowered tones of casualties, or food shortages, of my father coming home at the weekends after working nights in a munitions factory in Coventry; of going to Coalville with my grandfather's "man" in the pony and float, and queueing for margarine at the Maypole in High Street — about a mile and a half away. For about a year at the end of the war I went to a school run by refugee Belgian nuns in the old house before the bridge on Forest Road. I walked to that school and took sandwiches to eat at lunch time. But when the nuns were re-patriated at the end of the war I went to the County elementary school in Hugglescote.

We lived in a house in a three-storey block on Porter's Corner in Hugglescote, built by my great-grandfather John Porter in about 1880. There were two houses in the block, with my grandfather's Chemist shop in between. The house being built on a hill, there was a basement kitchen, a dining room on the street level, the lounge and two main bedrooms up a further flight of stairs and two more attic bedrooms above. All the heating was done by coal which had to be carried up the steep stairs in buckets, and the ashes carried down again in the morning. The cooking was done in the kitchen on an old black range. On one side was a boiler filled with water from the top, which was heated from the fire and drawn off through a tap at the bottom. On the other side of the fire was the oven where all the cooking and baking was done. The Sunday dinners were cooked in this way until I was well on into my teens. It was a tricky business maintaining the correct heat to cook the roast, the potatoes and the Yorkshire pudding all at the same time.

"Dig for Victory," Bridge Road School, Coalville, 1914-18.

We had two sources of water. One, the soft water, came from a pump over the kitchen sink connected to a rain water well out in the yard. This water was heated in kettles on the kitchen range for the washing-up, or in the boiler at the side of the range, and for wash days and bath nights in the copper built into the corner of the kitchen and heated by a fire underneath. The second source of water, for drinking, came from a pump out in the yard, and was shared with the house next door. All the drinking water was carried in buckets into the house. Water from this pump was also carried in buckets to the outside toilet, because although we were fortunate enough to have a lavatory connected to the main sewer, there was no running water to flush it. We had no tap water until I was a teenager, and then the days of bathing in a tin bath on the kitchen floor were over and a bathroom was installed in the attics. This was progress I suppose, and yet never have I tasted such cold and pure water as came from the pump surrounded by the pink rose bush, nor experienced again the luxury of bathing before a warm kitchen fire.

Most of our shopping was done in Hugglescote. On the opposite corner from our house was a general store run by the Johnson family, and they served our needs for many years. There were occasional trips to Coalville for special purposes, to Brown's in the High Street, for shoes, and sometimes to Lentons or Freeman Hardy and Willis, to Drewetts in the High Street for hats and material, sometimes to Onions and Whites for fish, though for many years we had fish from a man who came with a pony and dray from Ellistown (and he came down the hill at a spanking pace) shouting "M-a-c-k-r-e-l, fresh M-a-c-k-r-e-l". The milkman came round to the back door with his bucket of milk and a metal measure hanging on the side of the bucket. We provided the jug and the milkman ladled into it the required amount. Bread was also delivered to the back door. It was usual for coal to be transported by horse and cart and tipped in the roadway in front of the customer's house, and then he was responsible for moving it into his coal house.

At Christmas time there was the annual trip into Leicester. The night before the projected trip my mother made a list of what she had to buy for us and for my grandmother. It really varied very little from year to year. A brace of pheasants from the market, some candied fruit from Simpkin and James, a few cigars for this body and some handkerchiefs for that body. We would go on the train from Coalville station in the morning, spend the day in Leicester, have a fish and chips lunch in Winn's Cafe in the market place, and return in the evening, walking in the cold dark night, sometimes from Coalville, sometimes from Bardon Station. Occasionally we would make a trip to Whitwick to visit my aunt, or to Loughborough to go to a dentist. Then we would go from Hugglescote Station in the train with the basketwork seats, which had backs which swung back and fore so that one could always sit facing the engine, and could watch the engine driver exchanging staves with the porter or stationmaster on the platform, and watch the engine taking on water, just like Thomas the Tank Engine. Sometimes we went to visit my paternal grandmother in Coventry, and then too we went from Hugglescote station, changing at Shackerstone and Nuneaton, and going through stations like Stoke Golding and Higham-on-the-Hill, names which still have an aura of mystery and adventure in my mind.

We were always very conscious of the pits and the miners. One of my early memories is the early morning ritual of the men going on to the 6 a.m. shift. They passed our house in the darkness of the early morning. It was a kind of dawn chorus of hobnailed boots on the metal road. First a metallic sound in the distance, then a growing volume of clattering sound. Strangely I have no recollection of voices. Did they march in silence? But I do remember there was one who had a club foot and had to start before the main body in order to arrive in time. It was some time before the miners could afford bicycles. They always came home in "their black" of course and the only bath after work was a tin bath of hot water on the kitchen hearth before the range fire. However hard the wives worked to keep the houses clean they always had a smell of wet soot. There was the sulphurous smell too of the spoil heaps, a prominent feature of the villages and of Coalville itself. Whitwick pit bank always seemed to be on fire, glowing red in the darkness. My grandfather, though basically a chemist, also sold ironmongery and carbide for the miners' lamps. It was a time of poverty and struggle. Many a family depended on skimmed milk which the local farmers let them have cheaply, and fallen apples in the autumn were a welcome addition to the diet. At the time of the strike in the 1920's I remember my grandmother helping the local families with dinners, and I have been told that my grandfather supplied medicines to the sick without bothering about the payment.

There were however, the beginnings of the welfare state. It is difficult to remember at what stage the changes took place, one image fades into another like a surrealist film. But there were the beginnings of the NHS in my youth. My grandfather dispensed medicine for the local doctors. The customer came in with his prescription, the medicine was supplied and the prescription "filed" on a metal spike, and at the end of the day or the week these were sorted and sent to some office for payment. The medicines were pretty simple, one large Winchester bottle full of medicine for colds, another for indigestion. A good proportion of the doctors' prescriptions were sure to be these, and so large quantities of them were made up in advance ready to fill the patients' 8 ounce bottles. My grandfather also had one or two concoctions of his own. Many a baby was soothed to sleep by his "Infants' Preservative", and many a cough was cured by his patent cough cure called "Kof Klipper", though I suspect that the main ingredient of both was laudanum, a pretty strong opiate. My grandfather was also qualified to take out teeth, and this he would do in the back room of the shop, where he was just as ready and able to poison a dog!

High Street Level Crossing and Signal Box, Coalville, c1954.

One of the great events in our house was the coming of electricity. Until this happened, the lighting was by gas, with all the attendant difficulties of varying pressure, (how often did one hear "The light's poor tonight") of broken mantles, those delicate, intricate arrangements of gossamer threads, which had to be fired before they would work. In our house the gas did not go as far as the attics, and I went to bed with candles, for I slept in one of the attics. The coming of electricity meant not only better lighting, but also the great boon of a Hoover carpet sweeper. The days of lifting the carpets and hanging them over the washing line to be beaten were over. I suppose at about the same time came the "wireless". First there was a crystal set, with the "cat's whisker" which had to be manoeuvred into the correct position before one could hear the station. Then came the set which worked by battery, known then as an accumulator which had to be re-charged frequently, and which usually ran out just when there was a programme one particularly wanted to hear.

Entertainment of this kind, however, was minimal. Most of our leisure time was spent with friends. We walked, often over the Forest, or spent the evening in each others houses, doing embroidery, or knitting, or playing cards. In my aunt's house there were regular musical evenings, each friend contributing some part of the entertainment. There was the stationmaster with the good tenor voice, the disabled lady with a rather scratchy soprano, someone with a penchant for giving monologues. The repertoire tended to be repeated almost as often as the present BBC programmes, and consisted of the "Arab's Farewell to his Steed", and "George Washington and his father's cherry tree" variety. But the friendships engendered in this way endured over the years.

Christmas time was especially a time of parties, first in the house of one friend and then we all went to another friend's another night, until we had been to six or seven parties all within the same group of friends. They all followed much the same pattern and were much the same from year to year. There was a large meal, sometimes cold, but often hot, turkey and all the trimmings. The houses were mostly small but we managed twenty or so people with some ingenuity. Sometimes there were a few hands of whist to set the ball rolling, and after supper there were paper and pencil games, and usually at the end a session of charades. There were several people in our group who were quite gifted actors and the charades were of a high standard. The hostess always allowed the guests to make free with her wardrobe. At this time there was a family called Mr. and Mrs. Eagles who ran the Gas works in Hermitage Road, Whitwick, and they had several sons who ran superb parties. Their party was the highlight of the season. Within our group there was practically no alcohol taken, but I cannot think that there was any less laughter, and they certainly went on until the early morning.

By the end of the 1920s I had passed through the King Edward Grammar School and was off to the University. I took with me a very unsophisticated outlook on life, but a good grounding in the advantages of hard work, and experience of the ups and downs of industrial life which I have always been glad to have. When I returned at the end of the Second World War I was pleased to be back and to raise my family in the environment in which I had been born."

MR. ERIC JARVIS, another prizewinner, remembers his childhood in Number 92, Church Lane, Whitwick, between the years 1920-30. His memories recall the pulleys for drying the washing in the living room, fattening the pigs bought from the Monastery, and providing work for the women who sewed fancy patterns onto mens' socks.

"This house called 'Arnesby Cottage' named after the village where Dad was born in 1866. He came to Whitwick in 1873. It was a semi-detached dwelling, the first of its type to be built in Whitwick, built by a builder named Bill Orton in 1902 and bought by Dad in 1911. The youngest of 11 children, I was born there in 1914. It was a good sized 3 bedroomed house with an entry down the middle of the 2 houses with solid wooden gates either side at the top, and a six foot brick wall dividing the two yards.

It was in our yard in my early days that we threshed wheat with sticks, this wheat was grown on the "Navvies" allotment at the bottom of the Cemetery. Most of the corn was used for pig feed, and some to make 'Thrumity' which was wheat boiled and sugar and milk added, the taste of which was not to my liking, it was considered to be a poor man's food.

The boiling was done in a cast iron pot on the back kitchen stove; this stove was later replaced by a new type of stove called a 'Bonnie Bridge Dover' this was delivered to our house from Leicester by Charlie Shaw of Coalville who ran the 'Royal Mail Bus' at that time; he later owned 'The Greyhound' buses. This would be about 1922. The old black fire grate in the living room was replaced in the late 20s by a Yorkist stove that was bought from an exhibition in Leicester — a very fine affair with an open fire and a tiled oven with a warm grill underneath. This reminds me of the other two things in the living room; one was the pulley, purpose made for the Jarvis family. This stretched the length of the room and was triangular in shape and rods about 2 feet 6 inches apart which would take two full sheets as well as pillow cases for drying. It was let down and pulled up by a rope and pulleys at the side of the grandfather clock at that end of the room — unsightly perhaps but a great innovation for drying and airing clothes for a large family. There were quite a few people who had pulleys in those days but I don't think anyone had one quite as big as that. I think that it was made by Mr. Concannon who at that time lived in Church Lane. To do the washing, we always used the tub and punches. Mother always got up at 4 o'clock to light the copper fire and everyone had to do so much before going to school. We had two tubs, one to punch the clothes in and one to rinse. Of course, the whites were rinsed in blue water and then they were wrung out by the old upright wooden mangle.

In later years we had a mangle which folded down and made a table top. That was really posh for those days. The other thing in the living room was a wooden rack, 6 foot × 5 foot hanging in the alcove on the right side of the fireplace. This is where we hung 2 flitches of bacon after they had been cured. The other flitches were hung in a similar arrangement at the top of the stairs. The hams, which were of no mean size, were hung in the living room and front room. Perhaps not pretty pictures, not nevertheless pictures which nearly everyone was jealous of.

We were indeed fortunate to have a very good pig sty. Dad always bought 2 pigs about 10 weeks old early in the year, usually from the monastery. The pigs were fed first of all with bran which was scalded and added to little light swill. We had a very large oval iron pot which held about 2 to 3 gallons and the pig potatoes were boiled in it on the kitchen stove. When we got up the main crop of potatoes, we boiled them in the copper. When the pigs were small you had to be careful not to give them too many potatoes or you caused them to scour. When the pigs were older, you changed from the bran to what you called 'thirds' and then 'fourths' and in the last stage they were fed with barley flour — and that was for fattening. Of course there was always keen competition in the village as to who could get the heaviest pig. It was reckoned that the height of achievement was a 20-score pig, which is 280 lbs. On the inside of the pig sty was a loft which was where we kept straw and a few odds and ends and Dad put staples up there one day and sometime after he couldn't find them. He thought either Bartlett (my brother) or I had had them but we hadn't. When one of the pigs was killed its belly was full of staples.

There were many callers at our Front Room. Ever since I can remember it was a workroom and that's where we used to give the chevenning out. Chevenning was sewing fancy patterns on mens' socks, one on each side. There used to be a flower on the top of a long stem, then a foot at the bottom. These patterns were sewn with various colours of silk. Various firms used to send to our house 100 dozen or so of mens' socks and told Dad what pattern had to be sewn on them and in what colours. We would then send this work out to women, or they would collect it, one or two dozen pairs each. They would be given the appropriate silks and return the work in a limited time. I think there were about 50 women who worked for us — strangely enough most of them were Methodists. All the sewing was handed out from this work room in which were kept the hampers and the parcels and also a three-legged round table on which stood a winder. This winder was a home made thing — Dad made it. There were two uprights and drum on it made out of old wood — about eighteen inches in diameter I would think — a spindle at one end and a handle at the other. Now the circumference of the drum was just a needle full of thread. You probably wanted three needles of white and one of blue for each sock — probably 36 rounds and perhaps 2 rounds over. The silk used to come on bobbins and we used to wind it on these drums and cut it off and make it flat and give it out with the chevenning. Of course there were various patterns for the socks — JB1 and JB2, two of the patterns I can remember. The women used to get 1/2d a dozen for JB1 and 1/3d a dozen for JB2. We not only gave out chevenning but Dad used to have grizwalds out at people's homes. Grizwalds were home machines for making men's socks and stockings. A Mrs. Peters who lived at Thringstone next to the pub was one. There was also Mrs. Gunn who lived on Leicester Road and Mrs. Leyland lived on Foan Hill in Swannington. The yarn for the grizwalds used to come in hanks and we used to wind it on to the cones by the umbrella system. The yarn was a red and black mixture except when we used to make the socks for Whitwick Imperial football team, which, of course were black and white. My brother Bartlett and myself used to take the yarn out to these ladies and fetch them back when they were finished and it was always my job to press the socks or the stockings on a board. I used to get 3d a dozen for doing hose and 2d a dozen for doing half hose. Occasionally, we used to have a hamper of ladies' hose. They weren't dyed and we used to have to turn them — we got a farthing a dozen for doing that. We used to do this together as a family in the other room. Household tasks were shared out but it was my particular job on Saturday mornings to clean the shoes in the back yard. There would be anything from 10 to 14 pairs and they always included Dad's work shoes which he was most particular about and many a time he made me clean them again because they weren't quite right. And then in the wintertime there was always the addition of cleaning Dad's leggings with shoe polish. After the shoes I used to have to clean the knives and forks. They were cleaned first by pushing them up and down in the garden to get the worst of the dirt off and then you polished them off with emery paper. Another job was to clean the candlesticks which came out of the dark pantry. We used to clean the fat off with a knife and put the fat in a newspaper which was then used for fire lighting. The cleaning was then finished with scalding water and newspaper. Next came the "gerries" from under the beds. They were brought down from upstairs and they were always washed with hot soda water. Washing up after meals of course was a job for all children to share and I can remember on Sundays there was always a squabble who should wash and who should dry and who should put the pots away. Nobody like the job of putting away because you were last and you didn't get the best place beside the fire when you were finished. When I was older and the girls were at work I used to help Mother shake and turn the beds. We'd only got one flock bed at our house, all the others were feather beds and they were turned over every day. In this process of course there was a great deal of fluff and when it was upstairs cleaning day the hat boxes and everything else were absolutely smothered with the stuff. Every job had to be done on each particular day in our house come what may. We always washed on a Monday.

To conclude my life at 92, although a working life, it was also a time of play, which is another story, but all in all I had a very happy childhood."

---

MATILDA MIDDLETON was the oldest entrant to the competition, aged 94 years old. Sadly, she died in December 1987, but has left us her memories of Coalville, the nearby villages, and their characters. For her special contribution, the judges named Mrs. Middleton as prizewinner.

---

"Coalville is a mining town situated between Leicester and Ashby. There was two mines, the Snibston and Whitwick, but unfortunately these are both closed which caused a lot of unemployment and the families had to leave the district to get work which made trade bad. I remember a disaster at Whitwick about 1901 which caused loss of lives; it was a fire down one of the shafts. Coalville was not short of shops or public houses. There are three nice places of worship: Marlboro' Sq. Methodist (the Minister in my days was the Rev. Thomas Hartshorne); the Wesleyan Minister, whose name was Rev. Lampard; the Ebenezer, Ashby Rd., Minister Rev. Eatough. Each chapel had a Sunday School. I belonged to Marlboro'

Sq. On the last Sunday in April we had our Anniversary, sitting on a special platform and singing special hymns. We would all have new clothes on. In August we would have a treat which meant singing round the streets then back to the School for bread, butter and a piece of cake, then to a field to play games. We were given a bun and a bag of nuts. We then went home tired but happy.

There was two day schools, the Wesleyan (head master Mr. T. Frith), of which I was a pupil; the other was the Christ School. Later these were taken over by the Leicester Education Council. I remember dating my copy book for 1900 which made me feel old. There was not any electricity, so we would not have light; we had the old oil lamps.

The town has its own brass band known as the Coronation Band; my husband played a trombone. Until recently there was two engineering works, Stablefords and Wootons but now these are both finished. I can remember two Railway Stations, Coalville East and the Midland. These were our only way of transport, there were no buses or trams when they closed. Our streets were lit with gas; a man with a pole and hook connected it with a lamp and the light came on. Connecting Bridge Road with London Road over the railway lines were two bridges and, it was said a murder had taken place on one. Coalville Christ Church had a blind organist who was also a newsagent and never muddled his papers. Money was often scarce as the mines seldom worked a full week and there was not any dole.

Joseph Burgess and Son Ltd., Belvoir Road, Coalville, 1960's.

I remember an Elastic Factory on Belvoir Road; it belonged to the firm of Burgess and the manager was Mr. Farmer who lived at Forest Road. He employed a lot of girls who worked from 6 o'clock in the morning until 5 o'clock tea time and Saturday until mid-day; no half days. There was a greyhound track near the Half Way House, it was started by Sir George Beaumont of Coleorton Hall.

In the year 1893 when I was born my Father had smallpox and as there was not a hospital an old barn in a field was converted. Also a nurse was not available. My mother went, leaving my sister to take care of us, and I was the youngest of nine. My Father recovered and lived to be eighty one; his name was William Cory. I remember a family of Whetstone living at Broom Leys. We had not got a hospital so a womens guild started to work towards one by having raffles and bring-and-buy stalls. Then a Gentleman named Mr. Wooton offered to give us a thousand pound for each one we got, but the scheme fell through so our money was left in the bank. I am pleased to say we now have one being built, by now our money must have a lot of interest.

On Belvoir Road just up above Owen Street there was a farmhouse with a bare brick floor and people would go with jugs to fetch milk as there was not any bottles then. We knew it as Gutteridges Farm. The people living there was Mr. and Mrs. Vesty. Years ago before the road under the Mantle Lane Bridge went under the railway lines, it went level with them, which meant traffic was stopped while a train went through. When the "Times" printing works was in Margaret St. my husband worked there; he moved with them when they went to Bridge Road and stayed when he could have retired. He went errands and delivered parcels, as he could drive.

## Bardon Hill

Bardon is a village near Coalville. The work was in the stone quarry which is owned by the Everard Family who also live at Bardon Hall. There are a few scattered farms and a very old chapel known as Bardon Park. Its late Minister was the Rev. Haddon who lived at Forest House Lodge. There are two rows of houses with twenty houses ending in the old school which is being closed down by ringing the bell for the last time after 111 years.

## Swannington

A small place near Coalville where coal which has been put on the rail is taken up an incline in tubs and disposed of. There is a nice church known as St. Georges.

## Ravenstone

This village adjoins Coalville it has some very nice Almshouses given by Sir John and Lady Turner. Each Christmas the residents are given a present of money or a blanket. It has a nice church and the vicar which I knew was the Rev. Chatman. There was only a small front room shop where you could get a bit of chocolate or a few sweets; the lady's name was Mrs. Perkins. There was one Public House kept by Mr. and Mrs. Kendrick. Nearby is Snibstone Day School. The squire was Mr. Cresswell, whose daughter helped train Coalville V.A.D. class.

## Hugglescote

This place joins Coalville, it has a very nice church with a good peal of bells. It was governed over by Canon Broughton who was much liked. He visited everyone irrespective of their religion; he had a nice collie dog which went with him. If the dog lay at the house door you knew the Canon was in there. There is one Public House and the lady who kept it was Mrs. Harper. There was a good Sunday School with the Church and on Bank Holiday the children would parade and sing in the streets and return to a field and treats were enjoyed (it being Hugglescote Wake). There was a post office and a row of various shops. There was two ways into Coalville: up Belvoir Road which ends in the market place, the other is via Forest Road and ends on London Road. Years ago there was an old oak tree which was hollow and an old man who we knew as Grandad Brown would get in the tree and preach. There is now a nice day school, the old one of which Mr. Joe Garrat was headmaster is closed.

## Whitwick

This is an old Market Place, it has a very nice Catholic church and on the first Sunday in May the scholars have a parade to the image of the Virgin Mary in the woods. The girls are supposed to wear white dresses with veils. The Doctor in Whitwick is Dr. Burkett. There was a railway station but this is now closed. There is one day school and a number of shops."

## Social Life

Entertainment and amusements have changed dramatically over the last forty years. Perhaps some of the recollections below will bring back happy childhood memories for some readers.

ROSEMARY JARMAN lived in Belvoir Road, Coalville, in the early 1940s with her brother, sister and grandparents. She remembers a family wedding, Victory Day, and a trip to Blackpool.

"In the early part of the year we had a wedding in the family and my sister and I still talk about this wedding. Auntie Mary's wedding was a very special wedding — it was our first wedding, Auntie Mary died a few years ago, but we shall always remember her for her wedding. I think she left from our house to go to the church, they played "In a Monastery Garden". We came out of the church, after the wedding was over and I will always remember the smell of the carnations. We had a reception in the Co-op Hall in Marlborough Square. I remember my grandfather being put out because three cases of lemonade were flat, but what he didn't know was that my brother and I had been at this lemonade and took a cup full from each bottle and for each cup that we took out we had substituted water. We had a lovely reception, all the usual things, trifles and that. All the things came from Dunicliffes cafe, which I think was in the High Street, that was a cake and pastry shop, or pattisserie as we would call it today. That was a lovely wedding and reception.

Towards the end of the war, I remember Victory Day very well. It was a lovely day, peoples' lights went on and Christmas tree lights were brought out and put into the windows and Union Jacks put into the windows and people started to celebrate.

I remember the parade and the street party; Mr. Moore from the Halfway House dressed as a Dame and got a little drunk, someone reckoned that he'd thrown pound notes out of his window. How true all that was I don't know, but a few days later we found ten bob on the dog track, which we invested in food and pop with our friends. We all dressed up, there was a funny little shop that sold second hand clothes, we dressed up as all sorts of funny people, we had a lovely time. In the evening we had a bonfire and Jim Ellis, who was the local milkman, supplied a couple of his ponies so all the children could have rides.

I can't remember if we had a VJ Day celebration, perhaps we did, but it was eclipsed by the VE Day celebrations.

We went to Blackpool after the war, it was probably the first bank holiday after the war and we met lots of people from Coalville. It was then I saw the sea for the first time as far as I can remember. What I remember most about Blackpool is the smell of the fish and chip shops, it seemed to be full of fish and chip shops. We went to see Tessie O'Shea and Frank Randall and I think Arthur Lucan and his daughter — that's Old Mother Riley — it was all something to remember."

Park Road Coronation Street Party, 1953.

MR. D. SANDERSON, of Oxford Street, Coalville, recalls entertainment in the 1930s.

"There were trips which started from Coalville East Station on a Sunday evening which cost 2/6d which were very nice. I had just started to work at Woottons Iron Foundry and I recall the Horticultural Show, Beauty Queen, cycle racing, track events and the Greasy pole with a ham hanging from the top for anyone who could get it; there was a great turnout for these competitions. The Beauty Queen and Maids of Honour were paraded around the streets to Crescent Road. It was a brilliant day out — everything for all ages. This included being led by a comic band — they were very funny.

Fun fairs and Circuses were pretty often, and were mainly located on the field at Owen Street or on the Central field which is where the precinct is now. Also on a Sunday Evening either Snibston Colliery Band or Hugglescote and Ellistown played their music on Coalville Park bandstand, to a very nice and appreciative crowd. The old Palitoy building in Owen Street was used on a Friday evening for boxing tournaments and there was a full house every Friday. Eric Jones the Coalville's Southern flyweight Champion, used to fight especially one named Marsden from Nottingham. There were some good bouts, very exciting and something to look forward to."

LESLIE JAMES ROBERTS lived in Berrisford Street, Coalville. Along with many of the entrants to the competition, he clearly recalls the "big occasion in the Coalville calendar" — the "Co-op Treat".

"Children came from the surrounding districts and all the contingents assembled in Marlborough Square. The parade would move off with the local bands — Snibston Colliery, Hugglescote and Ellistown and others providing the martial music along Ashby Road up to the Co-op field in Ravenstone Road. I recall attending one of the "treats" and as it was in the days before throw-away plastic cups had been invented we all had to carry our own cups. Passing Snibston Colliery I was swinging my arms rather energetically when there was the sound of breaking crockery. All that remained in my hand was the cup handle. However, someone had spotted what had happened and had gone into their house nearby, brought out one of their own cups and replaced the broken cup. That was the spirit that existed in Coalville in those days. Arriving at the field we were divided into groups and for each party there was a large basket filled with individual bags of food. Cups of tea were plentiful (dispensed from large enamel jugs). The supply of boiling water was always organised by my uncle Albert Swain-Wardle ("Jolly" to his mates). He was assisted by a man named Saunders. All the water was heated in large coal fired coppers and it was no mean feat to keep the supply going for the hundreds of thirsty children. After the tea party most of us went to the fun fair in the next field to spend the extra pennies we had been given 'to spend at the Co-op treat.'"

L. G. WILSON of Central Road, Hugglescote brings to life the entertainments in Coalville between the wars.

"I was born on November 5th 1916, and my earliest memories were of the fairs and annual wakes in all the villages. Usually a band proceeded the parade, skittles, stalls, shys, etc. and dancing outdoors. Then we had the big fairs in Coalville. As children we were fascinated by the big steam traction engines which powered everything. The roundabouts, swings, gondolers, cake-walks. We heard all the latest songs on the steam organs, which were lit like fairy-land. Usually we walked round and round, unless you were fortunate to have a penny given you. But by now I was getting older and earning a penny or two running errands, collecting jam jars or bottles to take to the Co-op.

By now I'd seen the magic lantern shows in various chapel rooms such as the Baptist Chapel in Dennis Street, Hugglescote, also the Wesleyan Chapel (now Methodist) in Hall Lane now Station Road. Local concerts, male-voice choirs, drama groups all performed. Just after the Coal Strike in 1926, I would dash off to see the silent films at the Grand in Belvoir Road on the Saturday rush with my penny. Now I was hooked on this make-believe world on the silver screen. I, like hundreds of kids, couldn't wait till the following Saturday afternoon to see the serials and the cowboys and indians. It was pure magic. We'd see the writing on the screen, then boo and hiss the villain and clap the hero, and if you was lucky, leave behind a pile of monkey nut shells which you could buy with a (1/2d) half-penny or 1d penny. How I remember Mr. Perkins (THE ROCK KING'S shop) in Belvoir Road, Coalville; we had liqourice sticks, tiger nuts, coconut chips or a lucky bag to swell the afternoon treats. But by now the wonder of the age appeared in Coalville — talking pictures. I believe around 1928, I queued for ages to see the 1st (Singing Fool) Al Jolson, but was turned away, as the cinema was full. Eventually I managed to see this phenomenon. Everyone now flocked to the two cinemas owned by Mr. K. C. Deeming (Mr. Entertainment himself), the Grand, and the old Olympia (later re-named the Regal).

I'd left school at 14 and was working in a ladies shoe factory in Leicester, which incidentally I cycled to every-day in all weathers, often accompanied by other boys and girls in the same position as myself. Now I could go to 1st house Saturday nights cinema, and still be home by 10.00, (our parents were very strict in them days). The cinema was by now the Mecca for everyone. It was a meeting place, a courting place, a family place. Everyone seemed to meet there, young and old alike. The Olympia was far roomier than the Grand, and I believe had 3 prices, theoretically cheapest at the front, and dearer at the back. It even had double seats — a boon to courting couples. Now I was 16 I was allowed to go to the 2nd house starting about 8. Girls were interesting to us lads now, so we had monkey paraded up Belvoir Road by the Clock Tower into High Street and Hotel Street and back to see the talent. If you was lucky it could cost you 2 seats at the pictures, plus the sweets. But what great fun we had. Sometimes on my way home, (we all walked) I would go by the Jitty and have pennorth of chips from a static mobile shop outside Fr. Degan's Catholic Church in Highfield Street and listen to the dancers. This was it, I thought. He had several pens with live monkeys cavorting about in and coloured light bulbs. It was a wonderful sight, enjoyed by most of us. Now as well as this dance hall, we had the Baths Hall which was very popular. Many a time I've just stood and listened to the many good dance bands of that era in the thirties. Len Reynolds and the Metro, Billy Merrin and the Commanders, to name a few.

Mr. Deeming had this luxurious new cinema built, the Rex — over 1,000 seater. It was the latest thing in comfort and technology. Still as ever people were flocking in and it was our main source of entertainment despite television which had been invented, but very, very few could afford. Radio had always been popular, and the music halls were on the decline, especially in the big towns. So now from the 20s and 30s we come to 80s with colour tv's, videos, plus who knows what?''

Hugglescote Sunday School Treat, c1895, Halls Lane (Station Road).

WALTER HIGGINS O.B.E. J.P. now lives in Great Glen. He remembers an incident which will bring back memories for Coalville readers:

# The Coalville Carnivore

"A lion reported to be at large in Nottinghamshire in 1976 turned out to be a myth. But there was more substance in the Coalville lion which caused similar alarm some 63 years ago.

The scare started when Jack Hall, a well-known resident of the town, reported that he had seen a lion in a field adjoining Bakewell Street and Oxford Street at 2 a.m. Several sightings in the Broom Leys area were subsequently reported and it was thought the ferocious beast may have escaped from one of the travelling circuses quite common at that time.

I was a schoolboy at Markfield in those days. Coalville became a 'no-go' area and children for miles around were kept indoors after dark. Audiences dwindled at the Grand and Olympia cinemas; trade at the Fox and Goose diminished drastically; the town's market was virtually deserted after dusk; and a 'Coalville lion' costume won first prize at a local fancy-dress competition.

Sadly, my customary weekend trip to Bardon Hill to visit my maternal grandmother and receive her 'Saturday penny' was an early casualty, as were my visits to see my paternal grandfather and uncles at their High Street barber's shop opposite the station (haircuts twopence, shaves one penny), but a welcome bonus was the discontinuation of the journey to Alfred Noyes Jones, Coalville's professor of the pianoforte, for my weekly music lesson, which I much disliked.

Finally, an intrepid "Coalville Times" reporter, who like all newsmen was prepared to risk life and limb for a story, kept watch with a local policeman. In the moonlight a donkey was seen to go to a tub and lift its front hooves on to the rim in search of food. The nocturnal marauder which had terrorised the neighbourhood was only a peripatetic donkey, but the vigilant pair readily conceded that it looked just like a lion. It belonged to Joe Massey, a well-known local tradesman, and was apparently in the habit of wandering from its field after dark and returning after its escapades in search of tit-bits.

Thus was the mystery solved. Communications with Coalville were restored, and Joe Massey not only delighted in regaling visitors with the saga, but included it in his "Notes on Old Coalville" which I believe are still in the library's reference section. As for Jack Hall, he steadfastly refused to believe it wasn't a lion he had seen!"

## Shopping

Most of the entrants remembered the Coalville shops in detail, the arrangement of the goods, their prices and variety, and the characters behind the counters.

MRS. BARBARA FLISHER'S home was on London Road, Coalville. She describes a visit to the Co-op.

"Our nearest shops were the Co-op. The grocery and butchery shops were where the funeral parlour is now. At that time all the assistants were male. It seemed so clean as all of them wore white jackets and white aprons. We had Co-op numbers so you could draw or save your "divi". My gran's number was 500; my mum's 6415. You took your grocery list in an order book each week. The first item on ours I can remember vividly was 4lbs sugar 10d (the old pence!). This was weighed out into blue strong paper bags on big brass scales. Other bags were made very quickly by the assistants from flat sheets of white paper — twisted round their hands and tucked in one corner similar to our modern icing bags. There were no calculations except brains to add up the costs, but the men seemed to do it just as quickly as our modern machines. Monday was "penny bank" day too. The groceries were neatly wrapped in strong brown paper and string. I can remember too at the Central Stores the cash was put into a cylinder shaped box — screwed into an overhead attachment. A string was pulled and away went your bill and cash to the cash office and a few minutes later back came your change."

Familiar names can bring back many memories. OLIVER SPENCER takes us on a tour of the shops of Coalville, remembering many of the old family businesses, in addition to the larger, national stores of the 1920s.

"Although small shops abounded, we did have two which could be described as 'department stores', the Co-op in Marlborough Square, Belvoir Road, usually referred to as 'The Stores' and 'Pickworths' a row of shops in Belvoir Road not far from the Snibston New Inn.

Everybody's needs were catered for by old established firms, some of which had rather funny names, "Onions, White and Co." were fishmongers in High Street, whilst Danny "Sitdown" had his popular greengrocery next to the Royal Oak. The national multiples were along High Street, Maypole, Home and Colonial, Melias, Worthingtons, and a late comer in the early thirties of which we were proud was 'Boots', as also was Woolworths.

The projecting clock along High Street denoted a rather handsome Jewellers "Lashmores", which gave its name to Lashmore's Yard, a row of cottages behind it. Nearby was a large chemist's Lands where you could also buy fancy goods. In the previous generation to ours it had been Porters, offering in addition to chemists goods, ironmongery as well, but which had eventually moved to the corner of Belvoir Road — Vaughan Street there were other chemists, Guest — High Street also an optician, and Roughton, next to Currys in Belvoir Road, where in his very dingy dark shop you could be handed a bottle of medicine and also be given an evangelical message. Down that side of the road there was an optician, Owen Parry, whose shop was denoted by a huge pair of projecting spectacles. Next came Moss, another jeweller. This row of shops included Holmes, the herbalist, with a perpetual window display of beekeeping appliances, Sam Turner, sweets, Vendy the Dentist who would take your teeth out any time of the day or night for a shilling a time. At the end of this parade was Walker, (nicknamed 'Tricky') who sold nothing but biscuits.

Before you came to the rail crossing, another block which been the site of the Primitive Chapel, comprised Greenlees, Boots and Shoes, the India and China Tea Co. and "Evans for everything musical". Very true for you could buy copies of the latest popular hit, or any instrument from a pair of clapperbones to a grand piano.

Further down on this side, after the stately Westminster Bank, another row of small shops. One sold books, and here I started my Library by buying a (Hardback) in the sixpenny "Readers Library" edition, "Pilgrim's Progress". Here also was Bloor's with its window bedecked with every kind of pork delicacy, pies, faggots, brawn etc. It was so popular that when the adverts came on the local cinema screen, "Bloor's — All the best pigs go to Bloor's" it would be loudly cheered. The end shop next to the 'Engine' (Engineer's Arms!) was Morris's and as he was a picture framer, it was not surprising that his window displayed examples of his craft.

We had an old established photographer Goulson, he was in between the Grand cinema and Bartrams the greengrocer. Then the flourishing Co-op departments of drapery, men's outfitting and footwear. Opposite the Co-op was the sign of three brass balls, for we had a pawnbrokers, Dicky Whitford, who also sold jewellery. Occupying a commanding site at the junction of Belvoir Road with Jackson Street was Coleman & Sons supplying every need in ironmongery and furniture. Strange to relate one of the sons set up in opposition and ran a similar shop further up the road.

In the 1920's there was very little car traffic as most tradespeople used horse power, consequently two saddlers had plenty of business. They were Owen, opposite the Station, and Amos, at the corner of Owen Street. Opposite the latter was for a while a 'Penny Bazaar' selling all kinds of very cheap household goods.

Butchers were scattered evenly round the town, Lager was opposite the Police station, Ward at the corner of James Street, and Fryer next to the "Bell" in the High Street. When a firm called the "British and Argentine" set up a shop in Belvoir Road it was regarded with grave suspicion by the local butchers, as they sold "foreign" meat.

The "take away" food shops of our day were of course the fish and chips shops. They were mostly tucked away up side streets, and at least one in a converted stable. The most famous was Parkers next to the garage in Hotel Street. Here you could either take away 'fish and penneth' wrapped in newspaper, or else stay to eat on the premises. they even had a 'first class Dining Room' where for less than a shilling you could have a fish and chip supper with a cup of tea, and be waited on by a waitress. Incidentally many of these shops also sold hot peas, for which you took your own basin.

Coalville's shopping would not be complete without mentioning the market on a Friday. Everyone went to the market on Fridays from all the surrounding villages. You could pick up bargains of all kinds, clothing, greengrocery, fruit etc. The 'cheap Jacks' were augmented from time to time by sensational travelling fellows who either sold marvellous cures for various ills, accompanied by entertaining patter, or offered gadgets the like of which were never for sale in the shops. One remembers particularly, a very aged character who had a stall of herbs, and the equally entertaining 'Marks' who specialised only in oranges. In the early 20's the market was only in front of the Red House and the corner of Mantle Lane, but when the old Smithy which stood on the "Scrap Heap" opposite, came to an end, the market expanded onto this site, which in time became earmarked for the Clock Tower Memorial. What was opened up later on the other side of the square next to the Post Office became known as the "New Market".

The little shops offering every variety of goods and services together with Friday's market provided for nearly all our needs, anything beyond this necessitated a train journey to Leicester which could be both an adventure and a rare treat in itself."

The "Star Tea Co.," High Street, Coalville, 1900.

---

Particular characters stay in our memories. MRS. ANN CAPEL of Priory Lane, Markfield, can vividly recollect one of Coalville's many personalities.

---

"Mrs. Lashmore smelt like her shop — dusty, fusty, old and leathery. She sat like a withered bird of prey behind her glass-topped counter — still and waiting.

I was terrified and over-awed by the monastic silence and museum-like atmosphere of the shop near the Railway Crossing.

It was basically a jewellers shop, but I remember most the ticking of the large clocks on the shelves high above the counter and the silvery trays, tortoiseshell mirrors and china jam-pots displayed at what was my eye level from the age of about 7 upwards.

I used to stand rooted to the spot not daring to move or speak while people shuffled around whispering, leaning over the counter to the bird of prey — hands pointed together making a church-spire beneath her pointed chin.

She was terrifying. Her skin was pale and tight, her hair drawn tightly into a bun parted down the middle. The half-moon glasses used to reveal very small cold eyes. I distinctly remember she always wore dangly earrings — silver or jet. This fascinated me as it was something glamorous — not seen in middle-class houses — certainly not in the middle of the afternoon! Her clothes too were always black and yes she wore a black shawl which she kept hoisting up her shoulders, covering the numerous necklaces of dull silver and grey.

I am sure there was a Mr. Lashmore, but he is remembered as a shadowy figure appearing out of a dark hole at the back of the shop. Where this led — I often used to wonder. He was summoned to look at the watches brought in for repair but I never remember actually seeing him as a Man or a part of the Shop.

Once I ventured in on my own to buy my mother a cake-stand. We still have it. It has a silver handle and pretty frilly edged plates. How exciting it was when Auntie Hilda came for tea and it was covered in a doiley and small home-made cakes arranged on it.

I remember to this day the agonies of going alone into the awesome blackness of the shop, the choice of china tea-pots, cream-jugs in the shape of cows, and jam-pots with strawberries, raspberries or blackcurrants in fat shiny china blobs on the lids which had a hole for a jam-spoon to lodge in. There were marmalade jars and honey jars with bumble-bees crawling over them, silver dishes with filigree edges, silver sets of fish knives and forks in lush, velvet boxes. What choice!

The outside of the shop was just as imposing and awe-inspiring. I remember it as being painted black with fancy lettering in gold above the long windows. The most exciting part of the whole shop was the gap between Lashmore's and the adjoining shop. This was dark and cavernous. Lashmore's had further delights in this Aladdin's Cave, and I remember many an hour being spent in there either just looking or playing cigarette cards, true-dare a promise or hopscotch.

No other shop has quite such sharp memories for me, although vividly I remember the obligatory journey on the bus "down the town" on a Friday afternoon. The open air market at the back of the Red House (now the Steam Packet), crossing over to the "Big Market" on the other side of the Clock Tower. A trip to Woolworth's followed — a memory of bare polished planks, and large wooden edges to the counters where ladies presided as on an island — and out of reach.

There was another alley-way between Woolworths and Pickworths, an emporium of rolls of material, millions of buttons and rows of cottons and silks. Rugs hung from the ceiling, in between which brass tubes on wires sped around, eventually reaching a lady in a windowed box in the far corner. She would return these tubes down to the counter with much clanging and whirring. Our change would clatter out onto the counter which to us was a miracle and were always begging to watch the "next ladies" magic to be revealed.

A trip to Colemans was a fitting end to our journey. I remember boxes and boxes of screws, nuts and bolts piled high up to the roof like little rabbit hutches piled up. Brushes, pots, pans, fireguards, dog irons, tools, bowls — everything higher and higher up to the ceiling where hung watering cans, tin baths, hoses, coke hods and shovels.

Our shopping completed, my day would be complete if a train was coming, the big white crossing gates were shut and a trip over the footbridge was suggested."

Marlborough Square, Coalville, 1930.

## Work

The nature of work fifty years ago was quite different from today; long hours, usually six days a week, for low wages. Most people started work when they left school at fourteen, to supplement the family income.

---

S. M. LEE of London Road, Coalville, writes about her work as a G.P. in Coalville. She provides an insight into the changes brought about by the introduction of the National Health Service.

---

"The winter of 1946-47 was one to be remembered — icy winds, deep snow-drifts, for week after week after week. Not the best of times to be initiated into General Practice, straight from warm hospital wards and over-heated surgical theatres. Cars, even with tyre-chains, could not cope with the conditions, so we had to trudge through the snow on foot to every visit and wellingtons were hard to come by. On one such occasion we went together, one with a spade to dig a path up to the Ravenstone Turn where a patient was in labour, and the other carrying the heavy case of medical equipment. This was a Forceps delivery using 'rag and bottle' anaesthesia as was usual for home-deliveries in those days. Very few births took place in hospital and it was not unknown to have to deliver the mother by the light of a bicycle-lamp in a sagging bed with the family dog underneath it, and a toddler asleep in a cot in the same room. After it was safely accomplished the doctor was usually invited to wet the baby's head with a mug of steaming hot tea laced generously with rum or whisky. Once when we had got to this stage, a young Bardon mother said to me "I may have a big family" — it was her 6th — "but I can assure you, they are all love-babies, not beer-babies like some around here" — a very splendid observation! Ante-natal and post-natal care were woefully inadequate at this time and knowledge of contraception was practically nil. Some of us did our best to rectify this.

During this same severe winter we had a phone-call one night about 2 a.m. saying that an elderly man well-known to the practice had become confused and agitated and could he be given something to calm him. The caller was asked to come to the surgery where the appropriate medicine would be ready for him. The answer to this was "I can't get through to the surgery there's a three foot drift for miles — you bring it here". Obviously a one way drift! Practically every G.P. lived 'above the shop' in those days, so were always available at all times and were expected to be so. Most medications were in liquid form, dispensed from large Winchesters or from very splendid Tincture bottles with ground-glass stoppers — the very same that command high prices in antique-shops today. We added a little bit of this, and a little bit of that — a veritable cocktail — and doctor's medicine was reputed to have a much higher cure rate than the more orthodox chemists' bottle, (my apologies to my colleagues in the Pharmacy profession).

Before 1948 when the N.H.S. came into being, every practice had these types of patient, (1) those who paid fully for services and medicines, (2) those on National Insurance who obtained services and certificates free, and (3) those who contributed 4d weekly per family and this allowed their wives and children free services and medicines, excluding accidents and attendance at child-birth. This last category was known as being on such-and-such Doctor's Club, and a worthy Coalville lady had a full-time job collecting these dues.

The geography of Coalville was very different prior to 1950, and much of the population of the centre has moved to estates that have grown up on its periphery. Stone Row and Club Row are no more, and only one house remains in Mammoth Street. These three rows of small miners' houses ran parallel to each other and formed a tight-knit little community. Behind each kitchen-door hung a zinc bath, and behind each front-room door hung the best clothes of the daughters of the house, protected by a layer of fresh newspaper. Those of us blessed with all mod. cons. perhaps did not quite appreciate the effort it took for these same young girls to appear spotless in our surgeries, for spotlessly clean most of them were, in deference to the doctor who would be examining them. I seem to remember that Greenhill was the first of these estates to be built, starting with Northfield Drive and Maplewell. It was the jolting I had from being driven over this still unmade road to give a dental anaesthetic to a child of three years that started me off in my second labour, so I remember the date well! Incidentally this goes to show that female G.P.s only stopped working when they were actually in labour — no Maternity Benefit for us.

Central Field was the area on which the precinct and car park were built at a very much later date, and this was used as a caravan-site for itinerants. These 'travellers' as they liked to be called were invariably courteous, and usually wanted to hand over their fee for services before any had actually been given. We seemed to have had more than our fair share of calls from this area — usually during the hours of darkness - but found out later than we had had a secret sign put on our entry to indicate our willingness to oblige. 1948 and the inception of the N.H.S. was the big water-shed in our professional lives, as in that of all G.P's. On the whole it came as a great relief; no longer did one have to ask if a family could afford expensive but powerful medication such as the new antibiotics and anit-tuberculous remedies, but could simply write a prescription knowing that these would be dispensed by the local chemist at no charge to the patient. Many is the time previously that a family conference had to be held to see whether each member could contribute enough to buy these very expensive drugs. It was a relief too not to be required to send out bills. Doctors generally are not good business people, and often we used to be paid in 'kind', and not always the type of 'kind' that we would have preferred. It was the time when people used to keep a pig in their back-garden to eke out the rations, and there is a limit to the number of faggots one small family can eat!

Proper ante-natal and post-natal services could be given and immunisation Clinics began. Hospital and Public Health Laboratories began accepting our specimens; previously we had performed our own blood and urine tests and all this took time. On the debit side no allowance was made in either time or money for us to perform minor operations in our own surgery. We had been accustomed to set aside Thursday afternoons for this, and many is the sebaceous or dermoid cyst we had removed under local anaesthesia. There was a rather ancient Boyle's machine that one of us used for longer procedures whilst the other operated. I still miss these Thursday sessions, as I do much of the early days.

Only one thing is exactly the same — the down-to-earth solid worth and friendliness of the majority of the Coalville people."

---

MRS. J. ALBERY'S grandparents kept the Stamford and Warrington Public House on High Street, Coalville. She describes the preparations for "opening time".

"The day was a busy one in the 1920s. We rose about 7.30 a.m. Breakfast in the kitchen across the yard was bacon and tinned tomatoes and bread. Tea was the beverage, I, being a child, had tomato and bacon fat. The floor of the bar was swept, and fresh sawdust was sprinkled on the wooden floor nearest to the street entrance. Fires were lit in Winter in the bar, the back parlour and in Granny's "snug" (a room down the little corridor at the end of the bar itself). The long bar, running the length of the men's bar was cleaned down. Any glasses left from the night before were washed, dried and stacked in the long shelves. If the bottles of spirits seemed to be nearly empty new ones were fetched and opened. The large glass container for port was also checked; this held 1 gallon of best port, and was topped up (particularly at weekends) from a small wooden cask. While this was being done the long yard, and wide entry to the yard, were being brushed down with a large bass broom, and if necessary swilled with water to leave it clean and fresh. At the same time, the men's and ladies toilets were swilled out and well brushed with disinfectant. Lastly the red tiled passage leading to the bar was scrubbed until it shone, and anyone daring to step on it before it was dry was loudly berated. Grandma used to inspect everything before opening time at 10 a.m., and things not sparkling clean, had to be quickly cleaned again. One of my tasks at the age of four was to help to dust in the back parlour, as every helping hand was needed. The large room with tables at the side of the front entrance was only used busy weekends and holiday times.

When I was 3 or 4 years old, Grandfather died and Grandmother was allowed to run the public house herself, by the brewery. The mid-day meal, after the pub opened at 10 a.m. was taken in shifts, mother relieving Grandmother behind the bar, or sometimes the meal was not until 2 p.m. when the pub closed. Then a quick cleaning up of glasses, a wipe down of tables and bar top, and we could have a rest until 6 p.m. opening. Closing time was 10 p.m. Then, depending on how busy we had been glasses were either washed or left until morning. There was a small metal sink with two draining boards and a tap and drain under the bar top at one end of the bar for this purpose! A galvanised bucket of hot water from the boiler in the back kitchen was brought to really clean up the glasses as the beer made them quite sticky."

The "Fox and Goose," London Road (no date).

No memories of the Coalville area would be complete without reference to the mines. REG ROOME of Wills Close, Greenhill, collects his thoughts in a poem, "Old Tom".

# Old Tom

Tramping through the darkened street
With hob-nailed boots upon his feet
Along the road at a steady plod
The very road his sire had trod
Down the shaft or down the drift
Just another start of a working shift
Into the bowels of Mother Earth
With mining in his blood from birth.

There where it's eternal night
To search for coal by candle light
In a seam not three feet high
And the threat of danger always nigh
Creeping crawling chest all bare
Breathing in that putrid air
Gnarled old fingers torn and sore
As at that precious coal he'd claw.

Half blinded by the grime and sweat
That devils gold he had to get
Back into the stall from whence he came
Blinking in the candles flame
Then trying to get a bit of ease
With snap tin balanced on his knees
What have you got his mates would say
The answer's same as yesterday.

Squatting there upon the floor
He eats his snap from dirty paw
That old pit pony champs at its bit
And nuzzles round for his share of it
Up at last where there's bright blue skys
Hands held aloft to shield his eyes
Body wracked in a coughing bout
To try to get that damn dust out.

Each Friday week they'd gather there
For the wages they all have to share
His grimey face fills with dismay
As he counts out his meagre pay
Then with a sigh he turns his back
And sets off down that familiar track
There at the end of that well worn path
Is his own fireside and his old tin bath.

Now gone are the moleskins the muffler the cap
The usual garb of a coalmining chap
No more in the fields will this man be found
With his ferrets and nets and his faithful old hound

This grand old man of the days of yore
Alas is gone and is no more
For he belonged to a special breed
Who lived by some unwritten creed.

I've known him since my life began
He was my dad this mining man, Old Tom."

Miners' Cottages, Ashby Road, Coalville, c1958.

GEORGE W. KENDRICK was born in 1903 at Vaughan Street, Coalville. He attended the Primitive School in Jackson Street when he was five, and was then transferred to Bridge Road School. Here he describes his working life after leaving school.

"I left school in February 1916, when I was thirteen years old, to go to work at Stablefords. Work started at 6 o'clock in the morning until 5 o'clock at night, with half an hour for breakfast and an hour for dinner. Saturday was halfday, 6 o'clock till 12.00, for this I was paid 6/- per week with 1d stopped for Doctor Jamie. I didn't like the work there and, much against my parents wishes, I took a new job at Snibston Colliery, where I stayed for fifty two years.

The manager of the colliery, for my first eight years, was Mr. J. Boam, who was succeeded in 1924, by Mr. J. Emmerson J.P. When I first started to work at Snibston, I was given a "tally", I was now 631, this number stayed with me for all my working life until I left in 1968, when I was presented with the "tally".

I began work, with other boys and men, sorting stone from the coal. On Saturday afternoons, to earn a bit of pocket money, I remember going back to work with two or three other boys, filling the eight ton waggons with slack, for this I was paid 9d, which was my Saturday night out spending money. For 9d I could buy 10 Woodbines 4d, a bag of caramels 2d and a visit to the cinema for 3d.

When it was known that I had worked for a time at Stablefords Wagon works, I was placed under Mr. Edward Thornley in the fitting shop where I worked a drilling machine. I stayed on the Maintenance side of mine work for the next 51 years, progressing from fitter's mate through fitter, head fitter and eventually mechanical engineer for my last 24 years.

We never worked above three days a week, during the summer months, except during the First World War. In the winter months we used to work four or five days. Then the strikes came and the depression. I was involved in both the 1921 and the 1926 miners strikes. In 1921 we were out of work for twenty weeks and in 1926 we were out for thirty six weeks. There wasn't any violence or any picketing, but we went back to work, defeated and worse off. There wasn't then any holidays with pay, no rest days, no free coal and no welfare.

We never really recovered from the strikes until, on 1st January 1947, the mines were taken over by the National Coal Board."

Whitwick Colliery Disaster, 1898.

AUDREY SYKES was born in Whitwick. She remembers the Great Strike and how it affected the local community.

"The majority of men worked at Whitwick Pit when they were opened round about 1820's to being closed definitely round 1985-86 which was a good record. Many were the hardships and privations, large families, small wages, up early, miles to walk to work before they got down into the bowels of the earth. Many areas of underground were made by being packed into a cage and lowered to total darkness, lit by candles, and later by carbide (shookies) fastened to their helmets. In earlier times deaths were caused by earth falls, trapped men took ages to reach, many were injured. Great loss of lives were caused by a big fire. The heads, "owners of the mines" "got together with deputy speakers for the miners" for better conditions. Myself, I do remember the Great Strike. It was grievous to see rejected men at street corners, men united to walk for miles with no wear in their shoes, no food in their bellies. Only just think of the soup kitchens, opened once a week and the rest of the week a miracle to happen, to be able to afford any type of food to carry on. A most beneficiary to the people of Thringstone was Mr. Charles Booth. He helped to find work on his estate of Grace Dieu living at Manor Farm. Many of Thringstone miners and their daughters who were able to work, were placed "out service" where they were able to know what good food was, what caring people, fair and honest to all who were in service to them. Boys were employed too, in the stables, gardens, woods, trained to be pantry boys, valet and Butler. Many unknown gifts were sent to the poor and fatherless of the village of Thringstone. The first Community Centre to be established was in Thringstone, I believe, by Mrs. and Mr. C. Booth, they were wonderful workers for Thringstone."

## The War Years

Most people can recount their experiences of war, happy and sad. All remember the shortages, air-raid sirens, gas-masks, and how the conflict affected personal and family life.

During the years of the Second World War, CECILIA SEALS (nee Turner) lived in Whitwick. She was one of many who took in evacuee children during that time.

"At the outbreak of the Second World War, I had four evacuee children billeted with me. All sisters, the eldest was only four years my junior. Having no experience of children at that time, the first week was a nightmare, especially when I discovered they all had head lice. I spent nearly all one day washing their hair with Derbac soap, effective up to a point, but what really worked was the regular use over a period of Rankins Ointment, which unfortunately had an obnoxious smell. Success came eventually, I finally cleared them, and we settled down quite happily, until their parents took them back to Birmingham on being told that they would have to contribute a little towards their keep. The government was paying me the princely sum of twelve shillings and sixpence per child per week, so I was usually out of pocket. Then I had a London mother with three small children. She had two sons in the army, and when they came on leave and their father came visiting, our house was overflowing, but we managed. We had a common enemy and it wasn't overcrowding!

About that time I became a Fire Watcher, and patrolled the Lane, with a stirrup pump and a bucket, on the lookout for fire bombs. I never saw any, which was fortunate, as I had no water in my bucket!

The war years were austere. The blackout, combined with coal rationing, food rationing, petrol rationing, sweet rationing, and clothing coupons, didn't make life easy. We were asked on our honour to have no more than five inches of water in a bath, and children were growing up with only the merest acquaintance with a banana. When it was at last all over however, Church Lane was a blaze of light. Everyone pulled back blackout curtains, and switched on lights. Hedges were hung with jam jars containing lighted candles. It was like fairyland. We had a street party later on for the children, and we all helped to make it as memorable an occasion as possible. That was 1945.

I married my sailor, in 1946, and finally left Whitwick in 1949, but the memory of those candles in jam jars still means the lights of home to me."

Volunteers leaving Coalville, 1914.

MR. E. HAGUE of Ashby Road, Coalville, describes the town's reactions to the Second World War: a new roof for Pegson's, a scheme for advanced warning of air-attacks, and the formation of Coalville's fire-fighting team, and the Home Guard. He vividly recreates both the tragedy and humour of war-time.

"They were eventful, turbulent years; the world shattering years from 1938 to 1946. The war years which I spent working at Messrs. Pegsons, a firm which, in common with most other engineering concerns, was turning from the manufacture of artifacts of peace to the production of the implements of war.

During those early years the possible imminence of war was seemingly never taken quite seriously; perhaps, God willing, it would never happen. But there was little respite from the work in hand. Men and women toiled diligently round the clock intent upon the appointed task.

When war was eventually declared there was a holding of breaths and a skipping of hearts; an hiatus — an uncomfortable sense of foreboding. This was "It" we thought, and waited for this undefinable "It" to materialise. Speculation was disturbing to peace of mind. And nothing happened — at first. So it was 'as you were' and everyone slipped back into the old routine.

The Phoney War they called it, this strange unexpected failure of the expected. This Indian summer which delayed the winter of chilling savagery.

If there had been complacency it was finally and irrevocably shattered when Goering at last launched his all powerful Luftwaffe on its mission of death and destruction, those terrifying bombing raids under cover of darkness. Lying as we did on the flight path to Birmingham and Coventry the ears of the night shift were now turned to that easily recognised pulsating drone of the enemy aircraft and the warning wail of the siren high on the police station. People now came on nightshift with a real sense of apprehension and an understandable prickling of fear; and not only for themselves. I know that I thought constantly of my wife and baby daughter and the terror with which they awaited daylight and my welcome home-coming.

Air raid shelters had been constructed at the bottom end of Mammoth Street to which we all repaired when so instructed. Not only Pegson's employees but many of the residents of that street sought their congested safety. Yet there were times when these frenetic dashes were proved unjustifiable. Planes flying well to the North or South of us posed no obvious threat.

Eventually to avoid the unnecessary shutting down of machinery and evacuation of the works, a scheme of advanced warnings was devised. From some appropriately-sited observation post, signals were transmitted to the works (and I presume to all the other works in the area) which indicated the estimated degree of danger. Green signified the approach of hostile planes. Receipt of such a warning did not require us to take any action. Amber intimated the possibility that we might be overflown and those in charge of the procedure would stand ready to order a general evacuation should the signal change to red. When it didn't we all breathed a sigh of relief and got back to work. If, however, our worst fears were realised there was a hurried dash into the night and the shelters.

One remarkable example of war time expediency makes me smile as I recall it. It concerns the roof which covered the extensive machine shop and had done so for many years. In peacetime it still may have passed muster but now the multiplicity of gaps occasioned by broken or missing slates allowed the light to stream forth into the night sky providing a possible guiding beacon for the air-borne invaders.

To install a new roof and still maintain a regular night shift seemed at first to be two irreconcilable objectives. Stripping the old roof off and replacing it with the new would entail several days' labour. But without a roof it would seem impossible to illuminate the building during the hours of darkness — and you cannot manipulate machinery in the dark.

The solution was most ingenious. the whole workshop was transformed into what I can only describe as a shanty town. Around each machine was erected a frame to which was attached sheets of opaque cloth; operators were incarcerated for long hours in these stifling, tent-like structures. Walking down the unlit central gangway with the open, star-studded sky above and the long rows of shadowy cells on either side was a most eerie experience.

One of the tasks assigned to us was fire watching. We would ascend a tall, multi-storied tower and take up our position alongside the steel water tank which was perched at the very top. From this cold and lonely vantage point it was possible to observe and locate any conflagration that might result from the dropping of Butterfly bombs or other incendiary devices. Fortunately I cannot recall any such eventuality ever arising.

The affair of the fire brigade was reminiscent of the Mack Sennet comedies of my childhood. One of the directors was inspired with the idea of forming our own fire fighting team. Volunteers were invited and a small weekly payment offered as an inducement. With what I considered to be a sense of duty I enrolled as a member under the leadership of a chap who had had some previous experience as a part time fireman.

The team having been formed, regular practice sessions were organised and such was the enthusiasm generated that a commendably high degree of proficiency was attained.

Alas, we had our detractors; the chief of these, a second director, was extremely critical and obstructive, constantly expressing the view that should there ever arise the need to call on our services we would prove to be found sadly wanting.

But for one unfortunate circumstance I believe we would have effectively silenced this choleric Douting Thomas. Our Achilles heel was the water hydrant. Standing as it did outside at the corner of the foundry it was never free from the depredations of the young lads from Mammoth Street. To prevent their constant turning on of the water and flooding the area a chain and padlock were utilised to secure the handwheel in the closed position. Our honoured leader retained the key in his possession.

Determined to prove his point this Mr. Awkward persuaded our mentor to arrange a small fire when we were all on day shift (a night time exercise would have been extremely precarious). Then they would call us out and observe our response. Thus, in secret, a pyre of old, oil soaked wood was prepared and lit in an open place behind the company offices and the alarm sounded.

We responded with praiseworthy alacrity only to find to our dismay that the custodian of the key had inadvertently left that indispensible item at home. While he left in haste on his cycle to retrieve it, I scurried to the workshop in search of a hacksaw with which to cut the chain.

Sad to relate, when the valve was finally released and the scene of the conflagration reached all that met our despondent gaze was a heap of smoking ashes. Thus ended our fire-fighting aspirations.

With the possibility of an invasion being an ever present threat the Home Guard was formed to help in the task of repelling those who might succeed in setting foot on this Island of ours. Pegsons, in common with other establishments formed its own unit. Often maligned and ridiculed at first I believe this Dad's Army would have given a good account of itself if the need had ever arisen.

True, it was a raggle-taggle army to start with. Although uniforms were not too difficult to come by arms were another matter. The regular army had first call. Eventually a number of Canadian Ross rifles were obtained — it was the bullets which were missing!

We drilled and practised and passed proficiency tests; tried our hands at throwing Mills Bombs on a range behind Snibstone Pit; carried out night time manoeuvres and stood guard on the work's main gates.

Then one night we were called out to a spot somewhere approaching Bardon Hill. Being a stranger to the geography of the area I blindly followed my Home Guard colleagues to a field on rising ground surrounded by tall untidy hedges. The scene that met our eyes in the gloom and mist brought us suddenly face to face with the stark reality of a war we had previously only read or heard about in the newspapers or on the wireless.

One of our aircraft, it seems, had fouled some telegraph wires and crashed in that field. Debris and mutilated bodies were the mute witnesses of the tragedy from which none escaped. We mounted guard until the proper authorities could arrive to commence their investigations.

I remember too that we made six pounder anti-tank guns and twin anti-tank guns for use in the desert campaigns and some I believe were used in that ear-stopping bombardment with which Montgomery began the assault which finally destroyed the myth of Rommel invincibility.

I remember — but that's enough."

Whitwick Colliery Home Guard.

## Schooldays

Most entrants to the competition agreed that discipline was strict in the schools attended between the wars; but all remembered their teachers with fondness and respect.

---

MRS. RITA PRICE of Avenue Road, Coalville, recollects her early years at school in Bardon, and later in Hugglescote.

---

"My school life started in January 1939 at Bardon Church of England primary school. My mother used to take me, along with children who lived next door to us. It was a fairly long walk from Waterworks Road where we lived, to school, but the teachers expected us to be on time every morning rain or shine.

My first teacher was Mrs. Thompson, our headmaster then was Mr. Allen. Others were Mrs. Allen, the head's wife and Miss Dutton. All of whom were very nice and very strict, especially about behaviour and arriving on time.

When I first started school we had to take packed lunches as there were no school dinners. Morning school started at nine o'clock and we finished at four in the afternoon. We always had an assembly in the morning, then back to our classrooms for lessons. We didn't write on paper, but on slates. They made an awful noise as you wrote on them, some of us used to scratch the slates with our nails, but never when a teacher was in the room.

As I got older I joined in more school activities such as maypole dancing and singing. I used to long for the whistle at four o'clock, so I could get out in the fresh air.

When I was six the Second World War broke out and all us youngsters had to go to school carrying gas masks and play out with them hanging round our shoulders in a box. We had to have blackouts at the windows and my Dad, a miner, at night was an air-raid warden. Some neighbour had some evacuees to stay, these were from Coventry.

When I was eleven I moved to Hugglescote Secondary Modern school, which is now a primary school. There was a school bus for us and we were given bus passes as we lived quite a way from the school. Those who passed the eleven plus went to King Edward VII Grammar school, which is now Newbridge High School.

When the war ended in 1945, I was twelve years old and in my second year at Hugglescote. We said goodbye to the evacuees and missed them for a while. Now we had a huge street party to celebrate the end of the war, and had big bonfires and loads of fireworks on Guy Fawkes night."

Hugglescote Church of England School, 1911.

LESLIE JAMES ROBERTS lived in Berrisford Street, Coalville. He clearly remembers the schools of his childhood, particularly Broomleys in the years just before the Second World War.

"My schooldays started from the Belvoir Road house and my first few years were spent at Bridge Road School. Pupils will recall the school bell each morning. This was rung by the caretaker Mr. Wilson, a quietly spoken, pipe smoking gentleman. The school was always spotless and kept clean without lots of helpers that always seem to be in attendance these days.

The infant's part of the school was under Miss Lager and some of her staff come to mind — Misses Burton, Amos and Hardy. Others on the staff were Miss Davis and Miss Turner, Brian Glover and Roy Woolerton. Some years later Roy Woolerton became headmaster of Belvoir Road School.

Visits by the school dentist were hated by one and all. After his examination each pupil took a form home for the parents to sign giving consent for the treatment. Woe betide you if the answer was "No".

Playtime in the school yard was great — someone would produce a ball and there was a general kick about with most of the lads joining in. The girls, of course, were in a separate playground. One particular day we all looked skywards at a giant airship that was passing over Coalville. Some time later it was learned that an airship, the R.101 had crashed in France near a town called Beauvais.

In 1944 it passed through that town when the Allied Armies were rapidly advancing across Europe. Was it the ill-fated R.101 that I saw all those years previously?

The school scholarship examination was taken under the strictest of conditions. Desks were set out in the school hall and I think it was Mrs. Massey who kept an eye on all the participants as they struggled through their papers.

About 1935 a new junior school was opened — this was to the rear of the original Bridge Road School and those of us who had taken the scholarship had a few months there before transferring to our new schools — either Coalville Grammar, Broom Leys, Ashby Grammar or Loughborough College School. The first headmaster at this new school was Mr. L. Page and Johnny Goulding was my class teacher. Kath Shilliam was the only other member of staff I can recall. She lived in a college on London Road not far from the Leicester Hotel. The front room was used as a sweet shop by Kath's mum, and it was here that many of us on our way to or from Broom Leys would spend what little pocket money we had to spare on sweets.

Broom Leys!!!! A school noted for the discipline meted out by the late T. W. Hill. "The Boss" as he was known to his pupils was, despite his ruling with a rod of iron, highly respected. This was proved when the first school reunion was held. Old Broomleysians turned up from all parts of the country and one or two from overseas. I personally returned early from holiday travelling some 150 miles to my home — a quick change and into another car for the final 20 odd miles to be part of that reunion.

What a headmaster — he always stated that he remembered all his pupils by name. How true. During the course of the afternoon we presented ourselves to the Boss. My turn at long last came round — I said Roberts 1935-1939 Sir." His reply "Hello Leslie — you lived in Berrisford Street didn't you." This, after almost 40 years, was to me truly remarkable. It is a story which I am proud to relate whenever I get the opportunity. He was a great man and had a loyal and hard-working staff. To name a few — Howard Harrison (who I believe is still alive and living in the South of England), Ken Darby, Brad Ramsell, Henry Wills, Misses Blaney, Pickup, Goulding, Bellamy, Jones and Walker. Not forgetting of course Coalville's own Fred Forgham, singer, amateur actor, show producer — one of nature's gentlemen. One thing I remember about Freddy — if you were a wrong-doer and punishment was coming your way he would, if you wore specs, say "Remove your glasses, I'm going to box your ears." I wonder what the pupils of today would say to that."

All Saints School, Coalville, 1950.